Stay He

Staying Healthy

You can get sick.

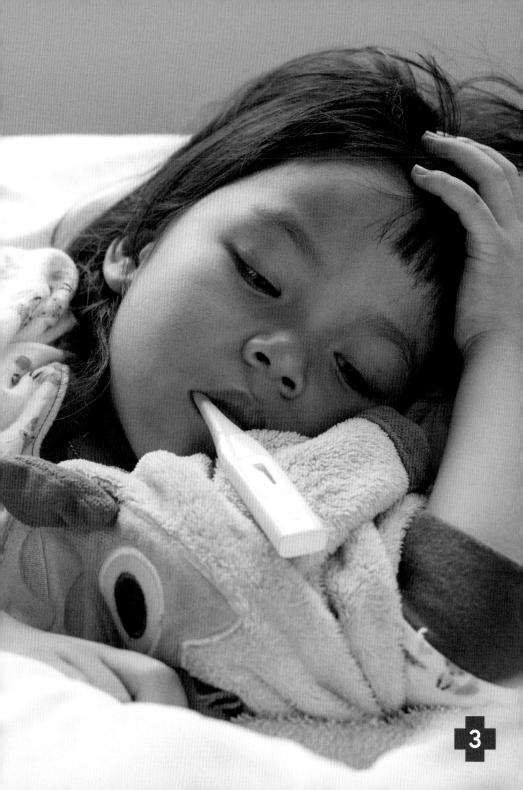

You can feel sick.

Your ears can hurt.

You can sneeze
and sneeze.

You can help your body to stay healthy.

You can eat good food.

You can drink water.

9

You can play games.

You can run.

You can jump.

You can

wash your hands, too.

We can all stay healthy!